EXPERIMENTS WITH ENERGY

A TRUE BOOK®

by

Salvatore Tocci

Children's Press®
A Division of Scholastic Inc.

New York Toronto London Auckland Sydney
Mexico City New Delhi Hong Kong
Danbury, Connecticut

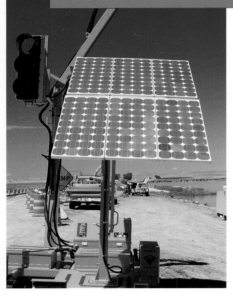
This traffic light is powered by solar energy.

Reading Consultant
Susan Virgilio

Science Consultant
Tenley Andrews

The photograph on the cover shows a windmill. The photograph on the title page shows the Whitehorse Dam in Yukon, Canada.

The author and publisher are not responsible for injuries or accidents that occur during or from any experiments. Experiments should be conducted in the presence of or with the help of an adult. Any instructions of the experiments that require the use of sharp, hot, or other unsafe items should be conducted by or with the help of an adult.

Library of Congress Cataloging-in-Publication Data

Tocci, Salvatore.
    Experiments with energy / by Salvatore Tocci.
       p. cm. (A True book)
    Summary: Explores the science behind energy through simple experiments that use everyday objects to demonstrate, for example, how food produces energy and how a roller coaster works.
Includes bibliographical references and index.
    ISBN 0-516-22786-6 (lib. bdg.)   0-516-27805-3 (pbk.)
    1. Power resources—Juvenile literature. [1. Force and energy—Experiments. 2. Experiments.] I. Title. II. Series.
TJ163.23 .T63 2003
531'.6—dc21

2002015257

CHILDREN'S PRESS, and A TRUE BOOK®, and associated logos are trademarks and or registered trademarks of Scholastic Library Publishing. SCHOLASTIC and associated logos are trademarks and or registered trademarks of Scholastic Inc.
1 2 3 4 5 6 7 8 9 10 R 12 11 10 09 08 07 06 05 04 03

Contents

How Can You Get to the Top?   5

What Is Energy?   8
Experiment 1: Doing Some Work
Experiment 2: Rolling Down
Experiment 3: Coasting Along

How Many Types of Energy
Are There?   19
Experiment 4: Burning Food
Experiment 5: Getting Warm
Experiment 6: Capturing Sunlight

What Are Fossil Fuels?   29
Experiment 7: Catching the Wind
Experiment 8: Falling Water

Fun With Energy   39
Experiment 9: Splitting Water

To Find Out More   44

Important Words   46

Index   47

Meet the Author   48

Funicular railways were first built in the 1400s as a way of getting people up steep hills.

How Can You Get to the Top?

Have you ever taken a train to the top of a steep hill or mountain? This type of train is called a funicular railway. A traditional train could never make it to the top. Its smooth, steel wheels would keep slipping against the metal track if the train tried to climb the steep slope. On a funicular railway, the train is pulled along the track by a thick cable. The wheels just guide the train up the mountain.

Funicular railways always have two trains that are connected by the thick cable. The cable goes from one train to the top of the mountain, where it wraps around a large, metal drum. The cable then goes down the mountain, wraps around another metal drum, and connects to the other train.

The drum at the top of the mountain is turned slowly by a motor. As the drum turns, the cable starts the trains moving. To understand how the trains safely make their way up and down the mountain, all you have to do is carry out the following experiments that deal with energy.

What Is Energy?

Almost everything you do involves **energy.** Running, walking, and sleeping all require energy. Some activities, such as running, involve much more energy than others, such as sleeping. What exactly is energy? Scientists define energy as the ability

When you are playing, you are using energy and doing work, even though you may call it fun.

to do some type of **work**.
But what exactly is work?

Doing Some Work

You will need:
- two empty 2-liter soda bottles with caps
- clock

Fill the soda bottles with water and tighten the caps. Hold a soda bottle in each hand by your sides. Slowly lift them straight up above your head. Time how long you can hold the bottles in this position. Relax your arms for several minutes. Slowly lift the bottles above your head again, but this time slowly lower them back down to your sides. Keep doing this for one minute.

You might say that it took a lot of work to hold the bottles above your head for as long as you did. However, scientists would say that you actually did not do any work.

10

To do work, you must use a force to move something. For example, you do work whenever you push or pull on an object. Scientists would say that you did work when you kept raising and lowering

A scientist would say that you are using energy to hold the bottles over your head, but that you are not doing any work.

the bottles. You used force to keep the bottles moving back and forth. In science, energy is the ability to use force to move something. How can you use energy to make something move without touching it?

Rolling Down

You will need:
- floor with smooth surface
- ruler with groove
- three books
- paper cup
- marble
- measuring tape

Set up your experiment on a floor with a smooth surface. Place one edge of the ruler on one book to make a ramp. Place the cup upside down and against the ruler at the bottom of the ramp. Place the marble in the groove of the ruler at the top of the ramp.

Make sure the cup touches the end of the ruler.

Flora of the Sea

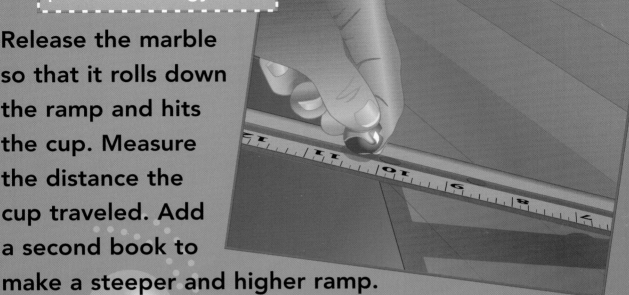

Release the marble so that it rolls down the ramp and hits the cup. Measure the distance the cup traveled. Add a second book to make a steeper and higher ramp. Repeat the experiment. How far does the cup travel this time? Add a third book and measure how far the cup travels again.

The cup travels the farthest when the ramp is steepest and the marble is at its highest starting point. The marble must have energy to make the cup move. But where does this energy come from? When you hold the marble at the top of the ramp, the marble has a type of energy called **potential energy**.

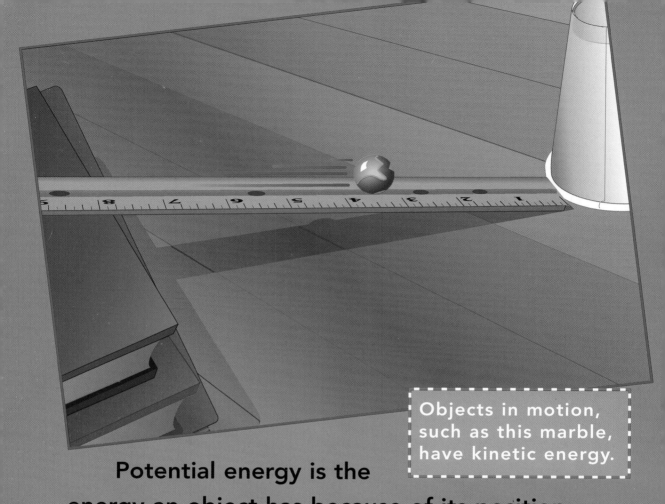

Objects in motion, such as this marble, have kinetic energy.

Potential energy is the energy an object has because of its position. Potential energy is stored energy that is waiting to be used. All objects that are not moving, such as a marble at the top of a ramp or water behind a dam, have potential energy. The higher you hold the marble, the more potential energy it has.

When you release the marble, it starts moving down the ramp. The potential energy that is stored in the marble is changed into another type of energy called **kinetic energy.** Kinetic energy is moving energy. All objects that are moving, such as a marble traveling down a ramp, have kinetic energy.

At its highest point on the ramp, the marble has the most potential energy. The marble has the most kinetic energy when it hits the cup and moves it the farthest distance.

The train of a funicular railway sitting still at the top of a mountain has potential energy. As it moves down the mountain, its potential energy is changed into kinetic energy that pulls the other train up the mountain. Can kinetic energy be changed into potential energy?

Coasting Along

You will need:
- masking tape
- 10-foot (3-meter) piece of clear plastic tubing
- flat wall surface
- steel ball bearing small enough to fit inside tubing
- watch or clock that can measure seconds

Tape the tubing to the wall to form a series of loops that go up and down. Make sure the beginning of the tubing is at the highest point. Place the ball bearing inside the tubing and release it. Does it come out the other end of the tubing? If not, adjust your loops so that it does.

Experiment with your roller coaster. What design allows the ball bearing to complete its ride in the shortest time?

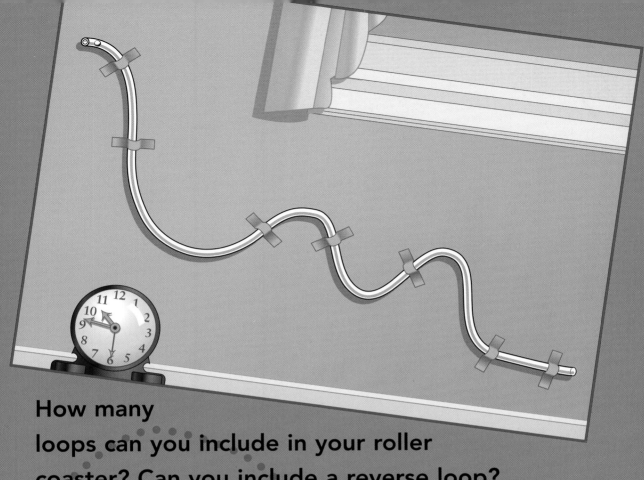

How many
loops can you include in your roller
coaster? Can you include a reverse loop?

You can ride a roller coaster because of the
changes that take place between potential and
kinetic energy. The cars have the most potential
energy at the top of each hill. As they zoom down
a hill, potential energy changes into kinetic energy.

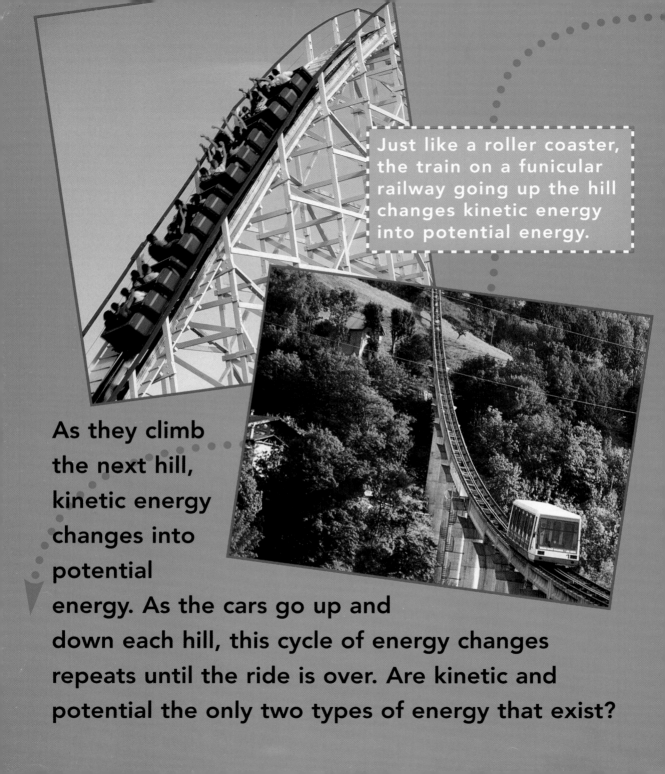

Just like a roller coaster, the train on a funicular railway going up the hill changes kinetic energy into potential energy.

As they climb the next hill, kinetic energy changes into potential energy. As the cars go up and down each hill, this cycle of energy changes repeats until the ride is over. Are kinetic and potential the only two types of energy that exist?

How Many Types of Energy Are There?

You have learned that you need energy to do work, which means using force to move an object. But you also need energy for everything else you do. For example, you need energy to think in school and watch television at home,

Watching television takes energy, but not very much.

and even more energy to
run and play. The energy for
everything you do comes
from the foods you eat. Is
there some way to prove
that foods contain energy?

Experiment 4

Burning Food

You will need:
- adult helper
- measuring cup
- small glass jar
- thermometer
- modeling clay
- straight pin
- peanut
- pencil
- paper
- matches
- tongs or oven mitt

Pour 1 ounce (30 milliliters) of water into the jar. Place the thermometer in the water. Make a small mound out of the clay. Stick the pin into the peanut. Then stick the pin into the clay. Record the temperature of the water in the jar.

Ask an adult to use a match to set the peanut on fire. As soon as the peanut starts to burn, use the tongs or oven mitt to hold the jar over the flame.

Hold the jar close to the flame. You can also try burning a marshmallow.

When the peanut stops burning, record the temperature of the water. The temperature rises. Foods, such as a peanut, contain a type of energy called **chemical energy.** When you burn a peanut, its chemical energy is changed into another type of energy called heat energy. The heat energy raises the temperature of the water.

When you digest foods, you use most of the chemical energy they contain to do everything you do. Some of the chemical energy in foods is changed into heat energy in your body. This heat energy keeps your body temperature from dropping when the environment around you gets cooler. If your surroundings get too cool, you may use still another type of energy to get warm.

Humans are known as warm-blooded animals because their body temperature stays constant even when the outside temperature is cool.

Getting Warm

You will need:
- adult helper
- fresh lemon
- table
- knife
- penny
- dime
- 6-inch (15-cm) piece of bare copper wire
- piece of electrical tape
- D-size battery

Shake and roll the lemon on the table. Ask an adult to cut two small slits in the lemon, about 1/2 inch (1.25 cm) apart. Place the penny in one slit and the dime in the other slit. Use your tongue to touch both the penny and the dime at the same time. Do you feel a slight tingling feeling on your tongue?

Now tape one end of the copper wire to the top of the battery. Touch the other end of the wire to the bottom of the battery. Does the wire begin to feel warm?

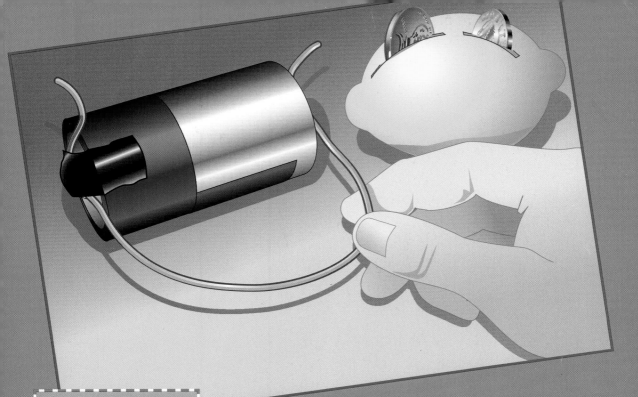

Make sure you remove your fingers from the wire as soon as it begins to feel warm.

The lemon acts like a battery that produces electricity. Like foods, batteries contain chemical energy. This chemical energy can change into another type of energy called **electrical energy**, which we simply call electricity. The tingling feeling that flows through your tongue is caused by the electricity produced by the lemon.

What you feel passing through the wire connected to the battery is heat. Where does this heat come from? Besides passing through your tongue, electricity produced by a battery can also travel through a wire. As it travels through a wire, electricity gives off heat energy, which makes the wire feel warm.

Many people use space heaters that are powered by electricity. Many people also use another type of energy to generate heat.

Heat is given off as electricity passes through the metal coils in the space heater.

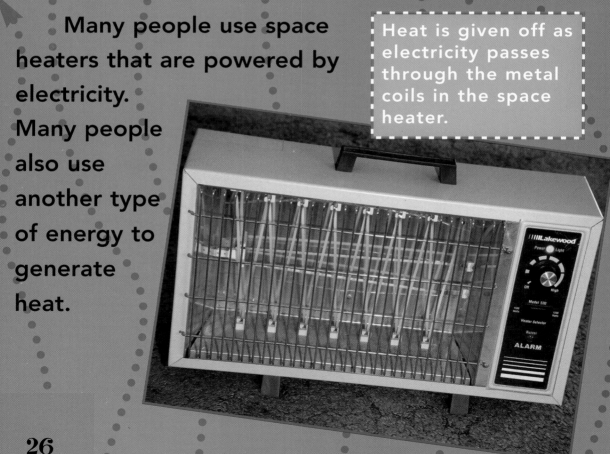

Capturing Sunlight

You will need:
- adult helper
- two empty plastic soda bottles
- paint brush
- black paint
- white paint
- two small balloons
- clock

Ask an adult to help you paint one bottle black and the other one white. After the paint has dried, place a balloon over the mouth of each bottle. Place both bottles in direct sunlight. Wait at least about fifteen minutes and watch what happens to the balloons. Touch both bottles. Does one feel warmer?

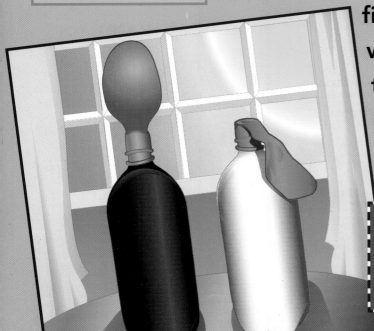

Stretch the balloons several times before placing them over the bottles.

The balloon on the black bottle inflates a little. Do you notice that the black bottle feels warmer? Sunlight is a type of energy called **solar energy**. A black object absorbs solar energy much better than a white object does. The solar energy warms the air inside the black bottle. This warm air expands, or spreads out, inflating the balloon.

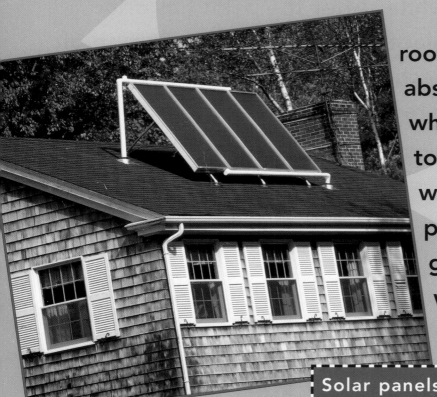

Some homes have roof panels that absorb solar energy, which can be used to heat water for washing. Most people, however, get their hot water by burning fossil fuels.

Solar panels are flat and wide so that they can capture as much sunlight as possible.

What Are Fossil Fuels?

Most homes are heated by burning a fuel such as petroleum, coal, or natural gas. These are known as **fossil fuels.** Fossil fuels are buried underground and were formed from dead animals and plants that became covered with dirt, mud, clay, and rocks. Throughout millions of years, pressure and heat slowly changed them into fossil fuels.

These fuels are used not only for heating homes, but also for powering cars, running factories, and lighting buildings. Most of the energy we use every day comes from burning fossil fuels. However, these fuels are limited in supply because they are being used much more quickly than they are being produced.

Most of the electricity and heat used in buildings comes from burning fossil fuels that contain chemical energy.

Scientists are trying to find other sources of energy for the future. One possible source is wind.

Catching the Wind

You will need:
- adult helper
- pencil with an eraser
- quarter
- 6-inch (15-cm) square piece of construction paper
- scissors
- tape
- 2-liter plastic bottle
- pushpin
- ruler
- string
- metal washer
- fan (optional)

Trace the outline of the quarter in the center of the paper. Make a cut from each corner toward the circle. Bend each corner to the center and tape them to make a pinwheel. Have an adult help you cut off the top of the bottle. Then cut two V-shaped notches in the top on opposite sides. Use the pushpin to attach the pinwheel to the eraser.

32

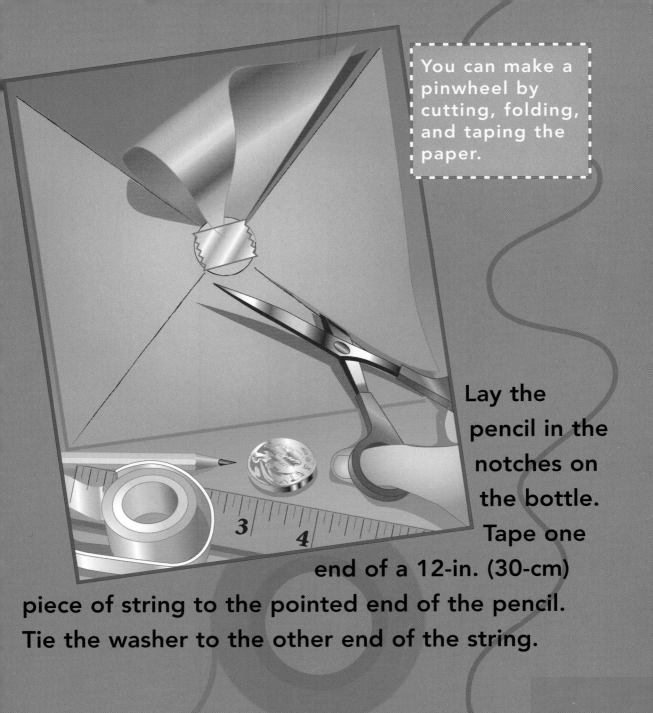

You can make a pinwheel by cutting, folding, and taping the paper.

Lay the pencil in the notches on the bottle. Tape one end of a 12-in. (30-cm) piece of string to the pointed end of the pencil. Tie the washer to the other end of the string.

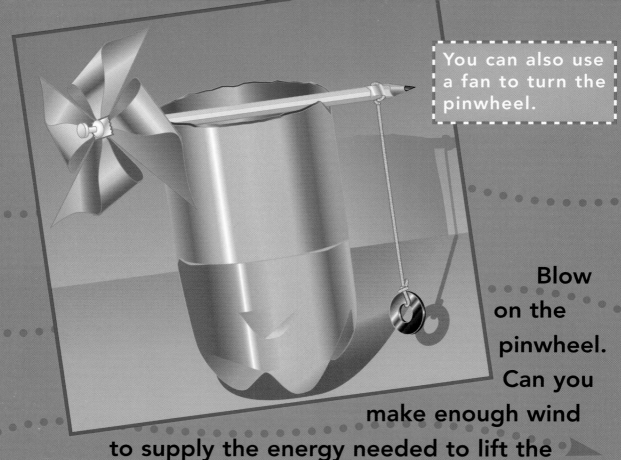

You can also use a fan to turn the pinwheel.

Blow on the pinwheel. Can you make enough wind to supply the energy needed to lift the washer? Experiment by changing the direction in which you blow on the pinwheel. Does one direction work better and lift the washer faster?

The device you made is a simple windmill. Windmills have been used to do work for a long time. Today, windmills are used in some parts of the world to produce electrical energy. Save the plastic bottle from this experiment to discover another way to produce electrical energy.

The windmills on the left use wind to grind wheat. The windmills on the right use wind to produce electricity.

Falling Water

You will need:
- adult helper
- large jar lid
- pencil
- cardboard
- scissors
- foam or plastic egg carton
- stapler
- pencil
- 2-liter plastic bottle
- sink
- ruler
- string
- metal washer
- small watering can or pitcher

Use the lid to trace two circles on the cardboard. Cut out the circles. Cut out several cup parts from the egg carton. Staple the cups in between cardboard circles to make a waterwheel. Push the pencil through the centers of the cardboard circles.

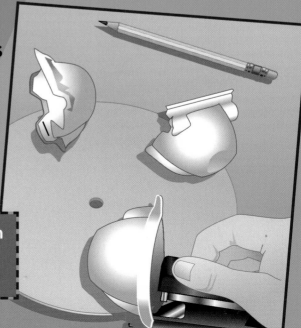

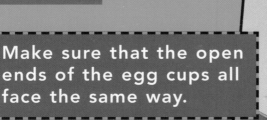

Make sure that the open ends of the egg cups all face the same way.

Have an adult help you cut the plastic bottle the same way you did in the previous experiment. Place both bottles in the sink. Lay the pencil between a groove on each of the bottles so that the waterwheel hangs between the two bottles and over the sink drain. Tape one end of a 12-in. (30-cm) piece of string to the pencil. Tie the washer to the other end of the string. Slowly pour water onto the egg cups. What happens to the washer?

Pour the water slowly onto your waterwheel.

Water makes these huge turbines spin to produce electrical energy.

The falling water supplies the energy needed to lift the washer. Dams use falling water to produce electrical energy. Dams funnel the water so that it causes devices called **turbines** to spin. The spinning turbines pro-duce electrical energy that is supplied to communities.

Fun With Energy

The trains on a funicular rail-way depend on the changes that take place constantly between potential energy and kinetic energy. The trains also depend on electrical energy to move the cable that connects them. This electrical energy probably comes from burning a fossil fuel that contains chemical energy.

Here's a fun experiment to see what you can do by changing the chemical energy in a battery to electrical energy. Heat energy from the sun or a stove will cause water to evaporate. However, see what happens when electrical energy from a battery passes through water.

Splitting Water

You will need:
- tall drinking glass
- teaspoon
- salt
- small piece of cardboard
- scissors
- two pencils
- sharpener
- two 12-inch (30-cm) pieces of copper wire with bare ends
- 9-volt battery

Pour warm water into the glass so that it is about two-thirds full. Add a teaspoon (1/6 oz or 5 grams) of salt and stir. Cut the cardboard so that it sits on the glass. Sharpen the pencils at both ends. Push the pencils through the cardboard, about 1 in. (2.5 cm) apart from each other.

Wrap one end of each wire around the sharpened end of each pencil. Connect the other ends to the battery. Set the cardboard on the glass so that the free ends of the pencils are in the water. Watch what happens near the pencil points in the water.

Do you see tiny bubbles collecting around both pencil points? The chemical energy in the battery changes into electrical energy that travels through the wire. This electrical energy then passes down the pencil and into the water. This energy causes the water to split into hydrogen and oxygen gases, which collect as tiny bubbles near the pencil points in the water.

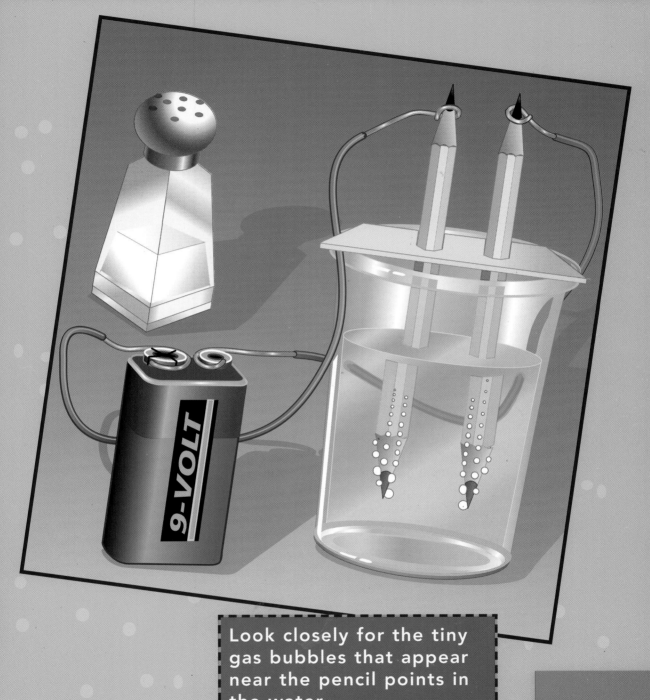

Look closely for the tiny gas bubbles that appear near the pencil points in the water.

To Find Out More

If you would like to learn more about energy, check out these additional resources.

Books

Fowler, Allan. **Energy From the Sun.** Children's Press, 1998.

Hewitt, Sally. **Full of Energy.** Children's Press, 1998.

Miller, Kimberly. **What If We Run Out of Fossil Fuels?** Children's Press, 2002.

Murphy, Patricia. **Push and Pull.** Children's Press, 2002.

Snedden, Robert. **Energy Alternatives.** Heinemann Library, 2001.

White, Larry. **Energy: Simple Experiments for Young Scientists.** Econo-Clad Books, 1999.

Organizations and Online Sites

American Wind Energy Association
122 C Street, NW
Suite 380
Washington, DC 20001
202-383-3500
http://www.awea.org/

Click on "Wind Energy Projects" to find out if your state is using wind energy to generate electricity for homes and businesses. An online bookstore has information about wind energy.

California Energy Commission
http://www.energyquest.ca.gov/index.html/

Click on "Art Contest" to see if you can come up with a drawing about energy that will be featured on a calendar, or check out "Saving Energy" to learn how you can conserve energy and save money. These are just two of the many links on this site.

Explorit Science Center
3141 5th Street
PO Box 1288
Davis, CA 95617
530-756-0191
http://www.explorit.org/science/energy.html/

Read the answers to thirty-one commonly asked questions about energy, such as "What is the most important source of energy for Earth?" and "Do we need to conserve energy?"

National Science Teachers Association
1840 Wilson Boulevard
Arlington, VA 22201-3000
703-243-7100
http://www.nsta.org/energy/findtop.html

This site contains a lot of information on energy, including a section on how our sun supplies us with energy through plants. You can also find out how we get energy from fossil fuels.

Important Words

chemical energy the type of energy found in foods

electrical energy the type of energy that passes along a metal wire

energy the ability to do some type of work

fossil fuel petroleum, oil, or natural gas that can be burned to supply energy

kinetic energy the energy a moving object has

potential energy the energy stored in an object because of its position

solar energy the type of energy found in sunlight

turbine a device that spins to produce electrical energy

work the use of force to move an object

Index

(**Boldface** page numbers
   indicate illustrations.)

batteries, 25, 40, 42
body temperature, 23
bubbles, gas, 42, **43**
cable, 6–7, 39
chemical energy, 22, 23,
   25, 31, 40, 42
coal, 29
coasting, 16–18
dams, 14, 38
digestion, 23
electrical energy, 25, 35,
   38, 39, 40, 42
electricity, 25, 26, 31, 35
energy
   fun with, 39–43
   types of, 19–28
   what it is, 8–18
food, 20, 21–23, 25
force, 11, 19
fossil fuels, 28, 29–31, 40
funicular railway, **4,** 5–7,
   15, **18,** 39
gas bubbles, 42, **43**

gas, natural, 29
heat, 26, 31
heat energy, 22, 23, 26, 40
humans, **23**
hydrogen, 42
kinetic energy, **14,** 15, 17,
   18, 39
motion, 14, 15
natural gas, 29
oxygen, 42
petroleum, 29
potential energy, 13–15,
   17, 18, 39
ramp, 12–13, 14
roller coaster, 16–18, **18**
rolling, 12–15
solar energy, 27–28
sunlight, 27–28, **28**
temperature, 22
train, 5–6
turbines, 38, **38**
warmth, 23, 24–26, 27–28
water, 14, 36–38, 41–43
wind, 31, 32–35
windmill, 34–35, **35**
work, 9, 10–11, 19

Meet the Author

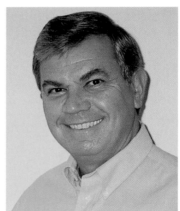

Salvatore Tocci is a science writer who lives in East Hampton, New York, with his wife, Patti. He was a high school biology and chemistry teacher for almost thirty years. As a teacher, he always encouraged his students to perform experiments to learn about science. He makes sure that potential energy changes very slowly into kinetic energy whenever he goes downhill skiing.